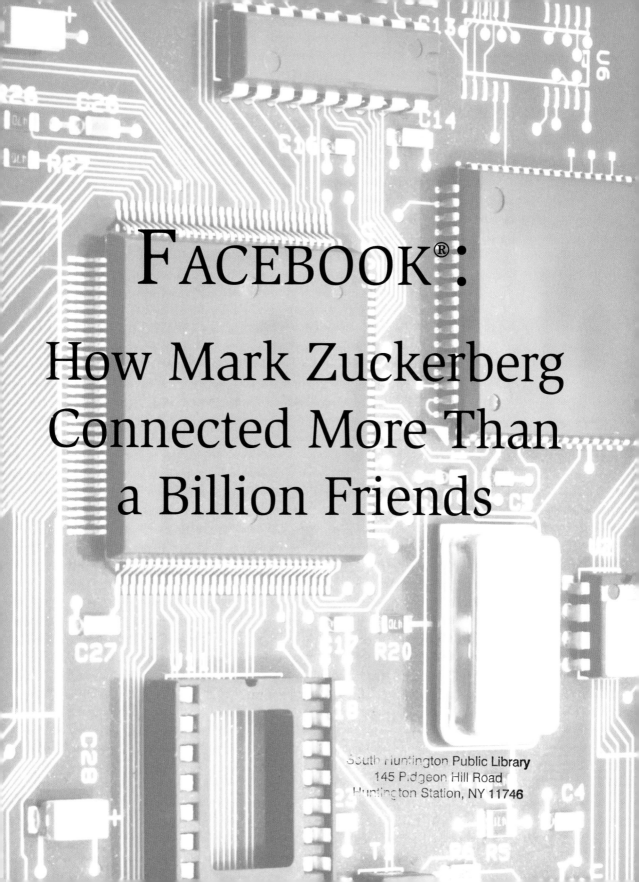

FACEBOOK®:

How Mark Zuckerberg Connected More Than a Billion Friends

WIZARDS OF TECHNOLOGY

WIZARDS OF TECHNOLOGY

FACEBOOK®:
How Mark Zuckerberg Connected More Than a Billion Friends

CELICIA SCOTT

Mason Crest

Mason Crest
450 Parkway Drive, Suite D
Broomall, PA 19008
www.masoncrest.com

Printed and bound in the United States of America.

First printing
9 8 7 6 5 4 3 2 1

Series ISBN: 978-1-4222-3178-4
ISBN: 978-1-4222-3181-4
ebook ISBN: 978-1-4222-8717-0

Library of Congress Cataloging-in-Publication Data

Scott, Celicia, 1957-
  Facebook(tm) : how Mark Zuckerberg connected more than a billion friends / Celicia Scott.
       pages cm. — (Wizards of technology)
  Includes index.
  ISBN 978-1-4222-3181-4 (hardback) — ISBN 978-1-4222-3178-4 (series) — ISBN 978-1-4222-8717-0 (ebook) 1. Zuckerberg, Mark, 1984—Juvenile literature. 2. Facebook (Firm)—Juvenile literature. 3. Facebook (Electronic resource)—Juvenile literature. 4. Online social networks—Juvenile literature. 5. Webmasters—United States--Biography—Juvenile literature. 6. Businessmen—United States—Biography—Juvenile literature. I. Title. II. Title: Facebook trademark. III. Title: Facebook.
  HM743.F33S36 2014
  006.7092—dc23
  [B]
                                                2014012227

CONTENTS

KEY ICONS TO LOOK FOR:

 Text-Dependent Questions: These questions send the reader back to the text for more careful attention to the evidence presented there.

 Words to Understand: These words with their easy-to-understand definitions will increase the reader's understanding of the text, while building vocabulary skills.

 Series Glossary of Key Terms: This back-of-the book glossary contains terminology used throughout this series. Words found here increase the reader's ability to read and comprehend higher-level books and articles in this field.

 Research Projects: Readers are pointed toward areas of further inquiry connected to each chapter. Suggestions are provided for projects that encourage deeper research and analysis.

 Sidebars: This boxed material within the main text allows readers to build knowledge, gain insights, explore possibilities, and broaden their perspectives by weaving together additional information to provide realistic and holistic perspectives.

Words to Understand

A *social network* is an online site for people to communicate and share information.

A *psychiatrist* is a kind of doctor who is an expert on diagnosing and treating mental illness.

Technology is the tools people have created to do work for them. Technology is becoming more and more advanced in the twenty-first century.

Computer programming involves creating instructions that tell a computer what to do. Computer programming can be used to create computer software like games or helpful programs used in business.

Computer *software* can describe any program that you use on your computer, whether a game or application used for work.

Potential is the possibility that someone may become something greater in the future than what he is right now.

A *prodigy* is someone who is very talented at something at a very early age.

A *passion* for something is a feeling of great interest and excitement for that thing.

CHAPTER ONE

Mark Gets Started

On June 8, 2010, the online *social network* known as Facebook did something far more important than connect "friends." It sparked a revolution.

That was the day when Wael Ghonim, a twenty-nine-year-old Google marketing executive, came across an image on Facebook that made him angry. The photograph showed a young man named Khaled Mohamed Said who had been beaten to death by the Egyptian police. Wael knew he had to take action. So he created a Facebook page. On it he wrote, "Today they killed Khaled. If I don't act for his sake, tomorrow they will kill me." He named the Facebook page "We Are All Khaled Said."

Today, Mark is one of the most successful people working in online business. He's changed the way people think about the Internet and created a hugely successful company. But he had to work hard to create the company that would change his life.

Two minutes after his Facebook page went live, three hundred people had joined it. That number climbed to a quarter million in three months. And then the voices on the Facebook page spilled out into Egypt's streets. Wael's Facebook page helped ignite the uprising that eventually led to Egypt's president resigning. It became a powerful part of the movement that's come to be known as the Arab Spring. Wael's willingness to speak out proved that one person can start a change that spreads like wildfire. But he couldn't have done it without Facebook.

"When you give everyone a voice," says Mark Zuckerberg, the founder of Facebook, "and give people power, the system usually ends up in a really good place. So, what we view our role as, is giving people that power."

That's what Mark has done through Facebook. He's given people all around the world a place to have a voice. And by doing that, he's helped to change the world in unexpected ways.

EARLY LIFE

Mark Zuckerberg was born on May 14, 1984, in the city of White Plains, New York. He grew up living with his family in Dobbs Ferry, New York. Mark's parents' names are Edward and Karen, and he has three sisters, Randi, Arielle, and Donna.

Mark's father, Edward, worked as a dentist in Dobbs Ferry, where his patients called him "painless Dr. Z" because of the gentle way he treated them. Edward's dental office was attached to the house where Mark and his sisters grew up, allowing him to work close to his family. Mark's mother, Karen, worked as a *psychiatrist* for a time, but she left her job to care for Mark and his three sisters. She also worked in Edward's dental office, helping him to run and organize his business.

Edward's dental practice exposed him to early computer *technology*, particularly when it came to X-rays and organizing his office. That experience with technology rubbed off on his son Mark, helping to shape

Mark was creating messaging programs that used the Internet for communication far before most people were familiar with getting online and chatting with friends.

his interests early in his life. Edward introduced Mark to ***computer programming***. He showed his son how to program using an Atari computer, an early, simple kind of home computer, much less powerful than the computers in our homes today. Mark learned quickly, and he soon found he loved computers and programming.

In 1996, Edward wished aloud for a way for his office receptionist to tell him that a patient had arrived in the waiting room. Up to that point, his receptionist had simply been yelling into the office, and Edward wanted something more efficient. Twelve-year-old Mark saw that a computer program could help solve his father's problem. He set to work to create ***software*** that could help.

The program that Mark built enabled the computers in his father's dental office and in the Zuckerberg house to send messages back and forth. Mark called his creation Zucknet. The program's name was a reference to Mark's nickname, "Zuck."

A year later, America Online (AOL) released its own messaging program, called Instant Messenger, but Mark had already seen the ***potential*** for computers to communicate with each other over the Internet. Zucknet allowed Edward's receptionist to send a message to him whenever a patient arrived. Using the program Mark created, Edward and his family could send messages between the computers in their home, as well. One night, Mark used Zucknet to send a gag message to his sister Donna while she did her homework. The message said that a computer virus would cause the computer she was on to explode in thirty seconds!

CONTINUING TO LEARN ABOUT COMPUTERS

Mark's parents realized their son had a gift for computer programming, so they hired a tutor to teach Mark even more. David Newman, a software programmer, began visiting the Zuckerberg home each week to

Mark's skill with programming was extraordinary for a young person, but also for a time in which fewer people owned and understood how to use computers.

teach Mark more about computer programming and creating software. When interviewed later in his life, Newman told *New Yorker* magazine that Mark was "a *prodigy*" when it came to programming. "It was tough to stay ahead of him," Newman said.

Mark started creating his own games, using his skills as a computer programmer. "I had a bunch of friends who were artists," he told a magazine interviewer. "They'd come over, draw stuff, and I'd build a game out of it." Mark loved to create new things through computer programming, whether games or new ways to communicate.

When Mark was a little older, his parents helped him take a college computer class at Mercy College, a college near the Zuckerbergs' Dobbs Ferry home. Each Thursday night, Mark's father Edward would drive him to the school and drop Mark off to attend the class. The first time Mark's dad dropped him off at the class, the teacher told Edward he couldn't bring his son inside with him. Edward had to tell the professor that it was his son who'd be taking the class, not him.

A BRIGHT STUDENT

Mark started high school at a school called Ardsley High School, located in Ardsley, New York. While at Ardsley, Mark studied hard and got excellent grades. He was particularly interested in Greek and Latin studies. Mark loved to read classical literature, and he enjoyed taking classes on the languages in which works like *The Iliad* and *The Odyssey* were originally written. By Mark's sophomore year, his family realized he needed more than what Ardsley High School could offer him, so Mark applied to a boarding school called Phillips Exeter Academy, called Exeter for short. Mark was accepted at Exeter, and he moved into the dorms at the Exeter, New Hampshire school.

At Exeter, Mark continued to do very well, both in school and in activities outside the classroom. He kept up his love of classical literature, Latin, and Greek. Mark also became an excellent fencer and became captain

Mark's Synapse Media Player was helping users find new music based on their favorite songs long before Pandora, Spotify, and other modern music services existed.

Research Project

This chapter introduces Facebook with a story about how the social media network was used to inspire a revolution in Egyptian. Using newspapers, magazines, or the Internet, find another news story that shows Facebook being involved in politics. Describe how Facebook was used in this instance to influence people's opinions.

of Exeter's fencing team by the time he graduated from the school. In addition, he won prizes for his work in math, physics, and astronomy, as well as for his studies in Latin and Greek.

Though he was always able to succeed in the classroom, Mark's *passion* for computers never took a back seat to his other activities. While at Exeter, he continued to learn more about computer programming and creating new software.

During his senior year, Mark created a computer program for his senior project called Synapse Media Player. Synapse was a program that recorded what kind of music users liked to hear, keeping track of the songs and artists they enjoyed. The program then automatically picked new artists, new songs, and new playlists for users based on the music they'd already picked. The website called Pandora.com picks music for users in a similar way, based on what they already like. At the time, however, Mark's Synapse Media Player was a brand-new idea. What started as a senior project from a high school student quickly spread on the Internet. Blogs and websites wrote about Synapse, and Internet users began downloading the project for themselves. To put Synapse into the world, Mark started a company he called Intelligent Media Group.

At Exeter, Mark continued to succeed in school and build his skill with computers. After graduating, Mark turned down a number of impressive job offers to go to college, where he'd create Facebook.

Text-Dependent Questions

1. Describe the role Facebook played in Egyptian politics back in 2010.
2. Explain how Edward Zuckerberg's profession influenced his son Mark to start creating computer programs.
3. What interested Mark most in high school, aside from computers?
4. What was Synapse Media Player?

Big technology companies started to take notice of Mark's program and the buzz that it was getting on the Internet. Soon, Microsoft and AOL were both trying to buy Synapse from Mark and offering him jobs creating software at their companies. Mark turned them both down and decided instead to go on to college after graduating from Exeter. Mark wasn't even eighteen yet, but he already showed great promise.

faceb

Words to Understand

Prestigious means important and highly regarded.

A ***fraternity*** is a social organization of male students on a college campus.

Hacking is using a computer to break into another computer's information by getting through the other computer's security programs.

Security involves the measures taken to stay safe from theft or other criminal activity.

Undergraduate students are college students who haven't gotten their degrees yet. Many universities have both undergraduate students and graduate students, who are trying to earn a second, higher-level degree.

If something is ***inevitable***, it is definitely going to happen; there's no avoiding it.

If something is ***controversial***, it causes disagreement.

CHAPTER TWO

Facebook Is Born

After graduating from Exeter, Mark decided to attend Harvard University, one of the best colleges in the country. When he applied to the *prestigious* school, Mark had plenty to put on his college application. He could speak and write French, Hebrew, Latin, and Greek. He'd won prizes for his work in many different subjects in school and been the captain of his school's fencing team. Mark had even created a computer program that resulted in job offers from two of the world's biggest companies, AOL and Microsoft. He was accepted to the school during his senior year at Exeter, and he began attending classes there in the fall of 2002.

COLLEGE LIFE

At Harvard, Mark began to take classes in psychology and computer science. He joined the university's Jewish *fraternity*, Alpha Epsilon Pi. At a

Though Mark didn't graduate from Harvard, the university played an important role in his starting Facebook.

party at the fraternity's house one Friday night, Mark met Priscilla Chan, whom he would eventually marry. Between classes and fraternity activities, Mark continued to create computer software, and he also started building websites.

During his second year at Harvard, Mark created a program called CourseMatch, which allowed users to decide on which classes to take based on other people in the class. He also created a website called Facemash, a very simple site that allowed users to see photos of two people and then vote on who was better looking. The site used photos of students at Harvard, which Mark got by *hacking* Harvard's computer network, taking pictures of students. In its first few hours online, a few hundred people visited Facemash.

Over the next few days the site was shared with people around Harvard, leading the school's administration to take notice and shut down the site. The administration was furious that Mark had gotten through the *security* surrounding their network. They threatened to kick him out of school, but eventually, they decided to let him stay at the university.

After Facemash was shut down, articles about Mark appeared in the Harvard student newspaper, and students were both outraged and interested in their fellow classmate. Soon, three students looking to start their own site came to Mark for help. Divya Narendra and Cameron and Tyler Winklevoss wanted to create a website that allowed students at Harvard to find each other online, share information, and possibly begin dating. They called the site Harvard Connection. Mark agreed to help Narendra and the Winklevoss brothers (two twins who were known to other students for their spots on Harvard's rowing team) in the creation of Harvard Connection.

STARTING FACEBOOK

Mark worked with Narendra and the Winklevoss twins on Harvard Connection, but it wasn't long before he stopped working on the site. Instead, he began work on his own web project, a site that allowed users to post

facebook

Facebook helps you conne
the people in your life.

Mark chose to use blue while creating Facebook because of his color blindness, but the logo and color became a huge part of Facebook's success.

information about themselves and see information posted by other students. He called his site TheFacebook.com, based, many believe, on the books Exeter gave students that included pictures, addresses, and phone numbers for every student in the school. "Face books" were a way for students to get to know each other at a new school, and Mark thought a similar idea could work online. Mark wanted the site to be easy to use and reasonably simple, so that anyone could use it. He made the main color on the site blue, because of his color-blindness; he can't see red or green. Blue was the color Mark could see most clearly, making the decision to go with blue and white an easy one. "Blue is the richest color for me," he later told an interviewer. "I can see all of blue."

In his sophomore year at Harvard, Mark launched TheFacebook.com as a way for students at the university to share information. The reaction from students on campus was very positive, and the site became quite popular. Students began sharing information about themselves, creating profiles and pages that explained their interests and contained their photos. Within one month of the site's launch on February 4, 2004, almost half of Harvard **undergraduate** students had signed up for TheFacebook.com and created their own pages on the site.

After the successful launch of TheFacebook.com, Mark worked with his friends at Harvard, Eduardo Saverin, Chris Hughes, and Dustin Moskovitz, to develop more ideas for the site. The friends had long talked about how the Internet would become more and more popular, until everyone used it. Looking back on his creating TheFacebook.com, Mark told an interviewer about his discussions with his friends:

> [We] would hang out and go together to Pinocchio's, the local pizza place, and talk about trends in technology. We'd say, "Isn't it obvious that everyone was going to be on the Internet? Isn't it, like, **inevitable** that there would be a huge social network of people?" It was something that we expected to happen. The thing that's been really surprising about the evolution of

Mark's earliest ideas for Facebook were based on sharing photos online. Mark saw that pictures would be a big part of social networking early on in Facebook's creation.

Before he started Facebook, Mark and his friends saw that in just a few years the Internet would become a huge part of everyday life, and that many people would want to share information about themselves online.

Facebook is—I think then and I think now—that if we didn't do this someone else would have done it.

Though the site began as Harvard only, Facebook soon expanded to other top-level universities, particularly with the help of Mark's friends Dustin Moskovitz and Chris Hughes. TheFacebook.com started to allow students from Boston University, New York University, Columbia, Yale,

At first, Facebook spread through Ivy League universities like Harvard. Students began posting pictures of themselves and sharing information online, and, soon, Facebook became hugely popular with these college students.

Cameron Winklevoss at the 2008 Beijing Olympics. The Winklevoss twins had a role in Facebook's beginnings.

Dartmouth, and Stanford to create their own profiles. Soon, the site became open to students from colleges all over United States.

By the end of his second year at Harvard, Mark was ready to drop out of college and run Facebook full time. Soon, the company would become one of the Internet's most successful, its website used by millions all over the world. But Mark's rise to success with Facebook wasn't without a difficult start.

CONTROVERSIAL BEGINNINGS

Despite the early success of Mark's Facebook.com, the site's beginnings were *controversial*. The students who worked with Mark for a little while on Harvard Connection believe that Mark stole the idea for Facebook from them. "[Mark] stole the moment, he stole the idea, and he stole the execution," Cameron Winklevoss told an interviewer years later. A few days after Mark launched TheFacebook.com at Harvard, Divya Narendra and the Winklevoss twins, Cameron and Tyler, told the student newspaper that Mark had told them he was helping to build Harvard Connection while working on his own site based on the same idea. They said Mark had lied to them about working on Harvard Connection and ended up taking their idea, leaving them with nothing.

Mark sees things very differently. He says that Harvard Connection focused on dating, while his site was based around the idea of sharing information. Mark has said that he created Facebook without input from the Harvard Connection project, despite the close timing of his working on Harvard Connection and starting Facebook.

Regardless of how Mark got the idea for TheFacebook.com, when the site launched, it quickly became a huge success. Though it started

Text-Dependent Questions

1. Describe how Mark got in trouble during his second year at Harvard University.
2. Why did Mark pick blue as the color for the Facebook site?
3. Why are the beginnings of Facebook considered controversial?
4. Why did Mark decide to leave college?

small it's reach grew quickly, and soon college students from all over the country were creating Facebook pages for themselves. With Mark leaving college, he'd have the time to focus on growing the site even more and creating what would become one of the Internet's biggest success stories.

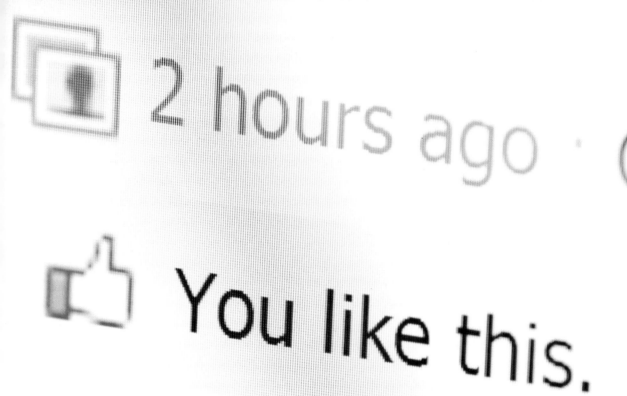

Words to Understand

Investors give money to companies in exchange for part of the money that company makes later.

When a company becomes ***incorporated***, it has the legal rights of a human being.

If something is ***gratifying***, it gives pleasure and satisfaction.

CHAPTER THREE

Growth

After the launch of Facebook in early 2004, Mark left college to focus on building the site and creating a company to help manage it. He was certain he didn't need a college education to achieve his goals.

To grow the new company, Mark moved to California, met *investors*, and opened up Facebook to new users. Over the next few years, Facebook would become one of the most important new Internet companies in the world, and the site's popularity would grow each year. New ideas and new users kept Facebook fresh and interesting, attracting even more people to the top social networking site.

Before the success, however, the company's first year began in a small house in California.

Sean Parker, creator of music-downloading program Napster, helped Mark make Facebook into the company we know today.

MOVING FACEBOOK TO CALIFORNIA

In the summer of 2004, with TheFacebook.com growing in popularity, Facebook *incorporated*. Sean Parker, the creator of the Internet music-sharing program Napster, had been giving advice to Mark about how to grow Facebook and start a company. When Facebook officially became a company, Sean became its president.

In June of the same year, Mark moved to Palo Alto, California, with a few of the friends who'd helped him start TheFacebook.com, including Dustin Moskovitz. The group rented a small house that served as the Facebook offices, as well as the home for the people who worked at the small company.

To start a new company is very difficult, but without money to pay for things like offices, computers, and the salaries of people who work at the company, it's nearly impossible. To keep Facebook going, Mark needed to find an investor who was willing to provide the company with some of the money he'd need to run the business. In the summer that Facebook moved to California, Mark, Dustin Moskovitz, and Chris Hughes met with a businessman named Peter Thiel. Peter is best known for having created PayPal, a system that allows Internet users to pay for the things they buy online using a credit card. PayPal had become a success with the increase in the number of Internet users shopping online, and Peter had started working to find companies in which to invest. Facebook was just the right kind of company for Peter's investment. At the meeting with Mark, Dustin, and Chris, Peter agreed to give half a billion dollars to the new company.

Now Facebook had the money it needed to continue to grow, and its founders were ready to work hard to make that happen. Mark and his friends had big plans for Facebook. Moving to California was just the beginning!

FACEBOOK GROWS

In 2005, Facebook bought the rights to use the name Facebook.com

Peter Thiel played a huge role in Facebook's early days by investing in the company before it was widely successful.

In 2006, Facebook opened to more users, expanding beyond colleges and high schools. The number of people using Facebook grew rapidly and the site quickly became one of the most popular social networking websites.

and changed the name of their site, losing "The" from the beginning of the name. In the same year, Facebook opened its site to high school students who wanted to sign up and create their own pages. (Before that, Facebook had only been open to college students.) Then, the company allowed the employees of a few important technology companies like Apple and Microsoft to join the site and begin sharing information about themselves. About a year later, in September of 2006, Facebook opened the site to anyone older than thirteen who had an e-mail address. From there, the company began to grow rapidly.

Mark introduces new features at the Facebook offices. Facebook has been able to keep growing by adding new features like chat, email, and games.

Today, Facebook is used in nations around the world, far from the website's start in a Harvard dorm room, and the number of people using Facebook continues to grow.

Just two years later, in August of 2008, Facebook.com had 100 million users. Mark took note of the achievement in a blog post on the site:

> We hit a big milestone today—100 million people around the world are now using Facebook. This is a really *gratifying* moment for us because it means a lot that you have decided that Facebook is a good, trusted place for you to share your lives with your friends. So we just wanted to take this moment to say, "thanks."

Research Project

Mark decided to move his company to California. This is where most of the other big computer companies were located. Use the Internet or the library to find out more about the history of this area in California, often referred to as Silicon Valley. Explain why this became the center for many growing computer companies. Why do you think Mark would have wanted to locate his company here too?

We spend all our time here trying to build the best possible product that enables you to share and stay connected, so the fact that we're growing so quickly all over the world is very rewarding. Thanks for all your support and stay tuned for more great things in the future.

One hundred million users might seem like a lot—and it is!—but that was just the start of Facebook's extraordinary growth. Only six months later, Mark posted on Facebook.com again, announcing that the site had reached 200 million people using the site. By early 2010, 400 million people had signed up for the site to share information and connect with their friends. A few months after that, in the summer of 2010, Facebook.com had half a billion people using the site.

Along with new users came more money for Facebook. In 2006, the company made just over $50 million, a lot for a new company, but very little compared to how much Facebook would go on to make. In 2007, the company made three times what it did the year before. By 2009, Facebook made three quarters of a billion dollars, and just one year later, the company brought in around $2 billion.

In just a few years, Facebook had gone from its beginnings in a college dorm room to becoming one of the biggest companies on the

Text-Dependent Questions

1. Why did Mark need to find investors for his company?
2. What role did Peter Thiel play in Facebook's beginnings?
3. After college students, which were the next groups of users allowed to be part of Facebook? At what point could anyone be part of Facebook?
4. Describe mathematically the rate at which Facebook grew in terms of number of members after 2008.

Internet. Mark's dream of creating a social networking site that allowed people from all over the world to share information about themselves with their friends and family had come true. He'd once made games and small programs in his parents' house. By 2010, he was running a company that many considered to be one of the most important of the Internet age.

Words to Understand

Applications are programs or groups of programs designed for end users.

A *lawsuit* is a disagreement between two people or groups brought to a court to be decided or settled.

To be *nominated* means to be selected as one of a small group up for an award.

If someone is *portrayed*, he is shown in some way through art, literature, a movie, or a play.

CEO stands for chief executive officer. A company's CEO runs the company and makes important decisions about what the company will do or how it will work.

Philanthropy is charity, giving money to others for the purpose of making people's lives better.

A *foundation* is an organization that is often nonprofit—in other words, it receives no money for the work it does—which works to meet specific goals to make the world better.

If you do something *anonymously*, you do it without letting others know it was you.

If two things are *conflated*, they get combined or mixed up with each other.

If someone is *passive*, she receives information or actions without responding to it in any active way.

CHAPTER FOUR

Challenges and Successes

In 2011, Mark Zuckerberg had a very special guest visit the Facebook offices. For the occasion, Mark took off his usual hooded sweatshirt and put on a suit.

When his guest saw what Mark was wearing, he grinned. "My name is Barack Obama," the visitor said, "and I'm the guy who got Mark to wear a jacket and tie. I'm very proud of that."

Not every company gets a visit from the President of the United States, but Facebook is no ordinary company. The company's website has changed the way people communicate, how people use the Internet, and the way people share information about themselves online. Mark and his company Facebook have been a leading force in the movement toward a more connected world.

Mark meets President Barack Obama, who spoke at the Facebook offices in 2011.

President Obama noted that Facebook was part of this global change as he explained why he had decided to hold an event at the company's headquarters:

> The reason we want to do this is because more and more people are getting their information through different media. Historically, part of what makes for a healthy democracy, what makes good politics, is citizens who are informed and engaged. And Facebook allows us to make sure this isn't a one-way conversation.

Facebook had made Mark the youngest billionaire in the world—and it had done a lot for the world as well.

NEW FEATURES AND NEW IDEAS

Facebook has changed a lot since it first began. Changes have helped bring new people onto Facebook and keep users who have been on the site for years interested in continuing to log on. One of the biggest and most important new ideas from Facebook has been Facebook Platform, which has helped spread Facebook's influence around the Internet and brought new features to the site itself.

Facebook Platform is a way for other companies and designers to use tools created by Facebook to change and add to the website. Using Facebook Platform, other companies can take advantage of the things that Facebook does to make what they do better or create entirely new uses for the social networking website. With the Platform, companies have created games that can be played by users and added other new ideas to Facebook, allowing users to do new things on the site.

By 2010, more than half a million *applications* had been created by companies and people around the world. These applications have also created new business opportunities for many companies. Zynga,

The Zynga game Farmville became a huge hit on Facebook and mobile phones, with millions of people playing with friends through social media.

a company that makes games for Facebook such as Farmville, has made hundreds of millions of dollars through their use of the Facebook Platform.

Facebook Platform also allows other websites to bring Facebook to their site. Users can now use Facebook features while reading their favorite blog or watching videos online on a different website. They can "Like" an article and have it show up on their Facebook profile. Users can see which of their friends have read the same article and see which other articles and websites they've shared. Facebook is now connected to sites all over the Internet, helping to make it one of the major ways people share information online. The site itself is also much more than sharing information or pictures, thanks to Facebook Platform bringing games and other features to the biggest social networking site on the Internet.

CONTROVERSY OVER FACEBOOK'S FOUNDING CONTINUES

In 2004, after Facebook had launched and become a success, Divya Narendra and the Winklevoss twins, Cameron and Tyler, filed a *lawsuit* against Facebook, accusing Mark and the company of stealing their idea for a social networking site that would connect Harvard students. The group of Harvard graduates, who had changed their site's name from Harvard Connection to ConnectU, said they deserved some of the money Facebook was making.

The lawsuit took four years to come to an end, and in that time, Facebook had become a giant of the Internet business world. To end the lawsuit against them, the social networking company ended up paying the founders of ConnectU $65 million in 2008. The $65 million was an amount based on how much Facebook was worth at that time, but not long after Facebook paid ConnectU the money, Divya Narendra and the Winklevoss twins said that Facebook had lied about how much it

Actor Jesse Eisenberg played Mark in *The Social Network*, earning positive reviews for his performance as Facebook's young founder.

was actually worth, and they wanted more money from the company. In 2009, a judge rejected that second lawsuit, deciding that Facebook was telling the truth and that Mark's company hadn't tricked the founders of ConnectU into taking less than they deserved.

The controversy over Facebook's beginnings was finally finished for Mark and his company. They'd paid the founders of ConnectU to drop their lawsuit, and that brought about an end to stories in newspapers and online that questioned whether Mark was honest about his company's start. But in 2010, the story about Facebook's founding would be told again, and in a way that it hadn't before.

MARK'S LIFE ON THE BIG SCREEN

In October of 2010, Columbia Pictures released a movie based on the first few years of Facebook called *The Social Network*. *The Social Network* tells the story of how Mark started Facebook at Harvard and turned the website into a successful company, while also focusing on the controversy surrounding the website's start and the legal battles Mark faced in the years after Facebook was founded.

The Social Network became a huge hit. The movie made more than $200 million around the world and was ***nominated*** for many awards, including Golden Globes and Oscars. In early 2011, *The Social Network* won more Golden Globes than any other film from 2010. The movie also won Best Motion Picture—Drama, an award that many consider the most important of the Golden Globes. At the 2011 Oscars, *The Social Network* was nominated for Best Picture, Best Director, and Best Actor, among others, but ended up winning Best Adapted Screenplay, Best Original Score, and Best Film Editing. People loved the movie!

The movie didn't paint the most flattering picture of Mark. In the film, he is ***portrayed*** as being somewhat dishonest, possibly taking the idea for Facebook from the creators of Harvard Connection, the Winklevoss twins and Divya Narendra. Mark wasn't thrilled that a movie about his

Aaron Sorkin won an Academy Award for his writing work on *The Social Network*. Sorkin has written for movies and television, including for television show *The West Wing* and the film *A Few Good Men*.

life made him out to be a disloyal friend looking to make as much money for himself as possible. "I just wished that nobody made a movie of me while I was still alive," Mark told a reporter.

The Social Network writer Aaron Sorkin based his script on a book by author Ben Mezrich called *The Accidental Billionaires*. The book told the story of Facebook's founding, but some critics say that the book is more fiction than fact. Mezrich didn't talk to Mark Zuckerberg while writing the book, but he did talk to Eduardo Saverin, one of the friends who helped Mark start the site. Eduardo was in the middle of a lawsuit against Mark during the writing of the book, but once that was settled, he stopped talking to Mezrich. After *The Social Network* came out, many of the people portrayed in the movie spoke up to say that the movie was a good story but not really based on what actually happened in the first few years of Facebook. "A lot of exciting things happened in 2004, but mostly we just worked a lot and stressed out about things," Dustin Moskovitz said. "It's just cool to see a dramatization of history." Writer Aaron Sorkin said that he cared more about making the story interesting than making it completely true.

Whether or not *The Social Network* gave an accurate picture of Mark and the founding of Facebook, it certainly helped make Mark more famous than he already was. In addition, the movie was a clear sign that Facebook had become a massive success. How many websites can boast that they have a movie based on their start? Mark and his website had become famous!

GIVING BACK

Mark also began to get involved with *philanthropy*. He understood that his success could be used to help others. By helping others, Mark was putting his success to good use.

In September of 2010, Mark announced that he would be starting a new *foundation* called Start Up: Education. The foundation's goal

Mark worked with New Jersey Governor Chris Christie and Newark Mayor Cory Booker to make sure students in the New Jersey city learn the skills they need for the future.

would be to improve the state of the nation's education system, with its first project being to work with the government of New Jersey to improve Newark, New Jersey's school system. Mark donated $100 million to the project, hoping he could help make Newark's schools an example to the entire country. Mark worked with Governor Chris Christie and Newark Mayor Corey Booker to try to raise more money to match the $100 million he was giving, all in the name of improving education for kids. Mark wanted them to have the same shot at a great education that he did.

At first, because of the timing of his donation just before the release of *The Social Network*, Mark wanted to give the money to help Newark's schools *anonymously*. Some people thought Mark wanted to give the money to make himself look better before the movie came out. They said he was trying to donate the money to get ahead of negative responses to the version of himself shown in *The Social Network*. "The thing that I was most sensitive about with the movie timing was, I didn't want the press about *The Social Network* movie to get *conflated* with the Newark project," Mark told reporters at the time. "I was thinking about doing this anonymously just so that the two things could be kept separate." Mark had to be convinced by Governor Christie and Mayor Booker to give the money publicly, without keeping his name out of things.

In addition to the money he put up to help the schools in Newark, Mark also announced in 2010 that he had signed the Giving Pledge, an agreement between some of the world's wealthiest people to give away at least half their money to charity over time. Billionaires Bill Gates and Warren Buffet started the Giving Pledge as a way to encourage the wealthy to give more of their money to charity, and Mark was eager to sign on.

FAME

Thanks to Facebook and *The Social Network*, Mark has become one of business's biggest names. His fame comes from the fact that he's still young, that he's become very wealthy, and that his site is one of the most popular on the Internet.

Mark played a cartoon version of himself on *The Simpsons*, lending his voice to an episode of the long-running show. In an episode called "Loan-a Lisa," the cartoon Mark Zuckerberg tells Lisa Simpson that she doesn't need to go to college to be successful in life. He tells her that he, Bill Gates, and Richard Branson all achieved their goals without the help of a college education and degree.

Mark visited *Saturday Night Live* when actor Jesse Eisenberg hosted the comedy show. On the show, Mark met Jesse for the first time. The two exchanged an awkward moment of silence while the audience laughed, before Jesse asked Mark if he'd seen *The Social Network*. Mark, dressed in his hooded sweatshirt, told Jesse that he did see the movie and that he thought it was "interesting."

The Facebook founder visited Oprah Winfrey's show in 2010 to discuss his $100 million donation to the school system of Newark, New Jersey. New Jersey Governor Chris Christie and Newark Mayor Corey Booker went on the show with Mark to discuss how they would turn around Newark's education system.

CONTINUING CONTROVERSY

Although Facebook has become one of the most successful Internet companies, many question whether its impact has been positive or negative. Some wonder whether Facebook.com has changed the way people communicate with each other in a way that makes relationships less meaningful. Others question Facebook's treatment of the privacy of its users.

When Mark was asked whether he sees Facebook as changing the definition of friendship for a new generation, making relationships between friends less meaningful, he replied that he believes Facebook has helped people become closer, no matter how far they may be from each other geographically. "[Facebook has] always had the goal of helping people connect with all the people that they want," Mark told *Time* magazine. Mark continued:

> Our mission hasn't been to make it so people connect with people that they didn't know. . . . It's just all about, you know, maybe you're not in the same place as your family or your friends right now, but you want to stay connected. I think Facebook gives people a tool to do that better, in ways they couldn't before. . . . What I think Facebook allows is for people to stay connected who aren't seeing each other in person everyday. . . . I don't think Facebook is taking away from any of the other interactions that you have, it's just expanding your social sphere so that you can keep in touch with all of these people. Before, you just wouldn't have had any way to do that. That makes people's lives just a bit richer.

When discussing privacy with *Time* magazine, Mark said that he understands that people's privacy online is very important to them. He believes in users' ability to control what information is shared and with whom it's shared, but he also thinks that sharing photos or information about yourself with friends and family can be rewarding and important to bonding with others online. Mark has said that openly sharing information is an important part of Facebook's mission, that making the world a more open and less secretive place is part of a change that the Internet—and social networking companies like Facebook—are helping to bring about.

Critics, however, argue that Facebook doesn't allow users enough control over their privacy. They maintain that Facebook.com doesn't give users the options they would need to keep some information from being shared with big companies looking to advertise their products to Facebook's users. These critics also say that Facebook's privacy options are

In 2013, Facebook bought photo sharing service Instagram, which allows users to take, edit, and share photos. Many believed the popular website and smartphone app would compete with Facebook, but now Instagram's success is also Facebook's.

too difficult to use or understand, and that these options change too often for the average person to keep up with them.

Though Facebook may have its critics, and debates over privacy and online relationships will continue, there's no questioning the massive change that Facebook and other social networking sites like it have helped bring to the world!

CHANGING THE WORLD

Facebook is now used by hundreds of millions of people around the world. It has become one of the most successful websites on the Internet today. The site has changed the way people view and use the Internet, transforming the web from something that ordinary people couldn't change to something personal. No matter who you are, you can have a page on Facebook that allows you to speak your mind, share photos of yourself and your friends, and tell others what you're reading or watching online. What was once a *passive* experience for Internet users is now something in which each person can participate.

In a recent survey, almost one-quarter of the time that people used the Internet was on social networking sites like Facebook. Considering that e-mail accounted for only about 8 percent of all the time people spent online, that's a lot of time on Facebook and other sites like it! Facebook was also the site that, on average, people spent the most time on per month. On average, Internet users spent around two hours per month on Google.com and Yahoo.com, around half an hour on Amazon.com, but more than seven hours per month on Facebook.com.

Smartphones have given people even more opportunities to access Facebook. It's the third-most popular app after e-mail and the web browser. A 2013 survey found that 79 percent of smartphone users check their phone within fifteen minutes of waking up. Facebook accounts for about a fifth of the time users spend communicating on their smartphones, which is just slightly less than texting.

Today, Facebook is more popular than ever, with a hugely successful smartphone app and hundreds of millions of users.

Research Project

This chapter indicates that Mark Zuckerberg is working to give back some of his fortune to the world, helping others who are in need. Using the Internet, find out some of the charities that Mark supports. How much money has he given away? How does he use his personal time to help others? What goals does he have for improving the world?

Facebook has also helped create a new vocabulary. When someone says, "I have to update my status because my friend just poked me after I wrote on his wall," she is speaking in the language of Facebook, a language that didn't exist just a few years ago. Facebook has become part of our culture in a way that few businesses and websites have.

Mark isn't done yet. He wants to change the world even more by getting every single person on the Earth connected to the Internet. To achieve that goal, he's started Internet.org. In 2013, he told *Wired* magazine:

Over the past few years, we've invested more than a billion dollars in connecting people in developing countries. We have a product called Facebook for Every Phone, which provides our service on feature phones; it has 100 million users. But no one company or government can build out a full stack of infrastructure to support this around the world. So you need to work together with folks. Since we've announced Internet.org, we've heard from operators around the world and governments who want to work with us. This is going to provide momentum to make this work over the next three to five years, or however long it's going to take.

Text-Dependent Questions

1. Explain how Facebook Platform is used. Why is it so useful?
2. How was the lawsuit against Facebook settled?
3. What is *The Social Network*? How did it help and/or hurt Mark and his company? Was it an accurate biography?
4. Why do some people criticize Facebook?
5. Describe how Facebook has changed the English language.

Mark Zuckerberg has become famous for the success he's had with Facebook. Today, he's also working hard to share his success with others and use his fame to inspire big changes in the world.

And despite all of his success and fame, Mark still wears hooded sweatshirts and t-shirts to work!

FIND OUT MORE

In Books

Beahm, George. *The Boy Billionaire: Mark Zuckerberg in His Own Words.* Chicago, Ill.: Agate B2, 2012.

Kirkpatrick, David. *The Facebook Effect: The Inside Story of the Company That Is Connecting the World.* New York: Simon & Schuster, 2011.

Maida, Jerome. *Mark Zuckerberg: Creator of Facebook: A Graphic Novel.* Suffolk, Va.: Bluewater Productions, 2012.

Mezrich, Ben. *The Accidental Billionaires: The Founding of Facebook: A Tale of Sex, Money, Genius and Betrayal.* New York: Doubleday, 2009.

Stewart, Gail B. *Mark Zuckerberg: Facebook Creator.* Farmington Hills, Minn.: Kid Haven, 2009.

On the Internet

50 Facebook Facts and Figures
www.facebook.com/notes/kuldeep-bhardwaj/50-facebook-facts-and-figures/10150274471574235

Mark Zuckerberg's Page on Facebook
www.facebook.com/zuck

Mashable: Mark Zuckerberg
mashable.com/category/mark-zuckerberg

The New Yorker: The Face of Facebook: Mark Zuckerberg Opens Up
www.newyorker.com/reporting/2010/09/20/100920fa_fact_vargas

Time Magazine: Person of the Year 2010—Mark Zuckerberg
www.time.com/time/specials/packages/article/
    0,28804,2036683_2037183_2037185,00.html

SERIES GLOSSARY OF KEY TERMS

application: A program that runs on a computer or smartphone. People often call these "apps."

bug: A problem with how a program runs.

byte: A unit of information stored on a computer. One byte is equal to eight digits of binary code—that's eight 1s or 0s.

cloud: Data and apps that are stored on the Internet instead of on your own computer or smartphone are said to be "in the cloud."

data: Information stored on a computer.

debug: Find the problems with an app or program and fix them.

device: Your computer, smartphone, or other piece of technology. Devices can often access the Internet and run apps.

digital: Having to do with computers or stored on a computer.

hardware: The physical part of a computer. The hardware is made up of the parts you can see and touch.

memory: Somewhere that a computer stores information that it is using.

media: Short for multimedia, it's the entertainment or information that can be stored on a computer. Examples of media include music, videos, and e-books.

network: More than one computer or device connected together so information can be shared between them.

pixel: A dot of light or color on a digital display. A computer monitor or phone screen has lots of pixels that work together to create an image.

program: A collection of computer code that does a job.

software: Programs that run on a computer.

technology: Something that people invent to make a job easier or do something new.

INDEX

ABOUT THE AUTHOR

Celicia Scott lives in upstate New York. She worked in teaching before starting a second career as a writer.

PICTURE CREDITS

Dreamstime.com:
6: Mohamed Hanno
8: Kobby Dagan
10: Warnerbroers
12: Gajus
14: Marcel De Grijs
18: Janaka Dharmasena
20: Jorge Salcedo
22: Sallyeva
24: Viorel Sima
25: Yanlev
26: Reinout Van Wagtendonk
30: Sebastian Czapnik
32: Sbukley
35: Anthony Brown
37: Slobodan Mračina

40: Tim Martin
44: Brandon Alms
46: Featureflash
48: Sbukley
50: Laurence Agron
54: Gary Arbach
56: Marcel De Grijs

16: Transmarinus at en.wikipedia
27: Johnnyroee
34: TechCrunch50-2008
36: Robert Scoble

93 95